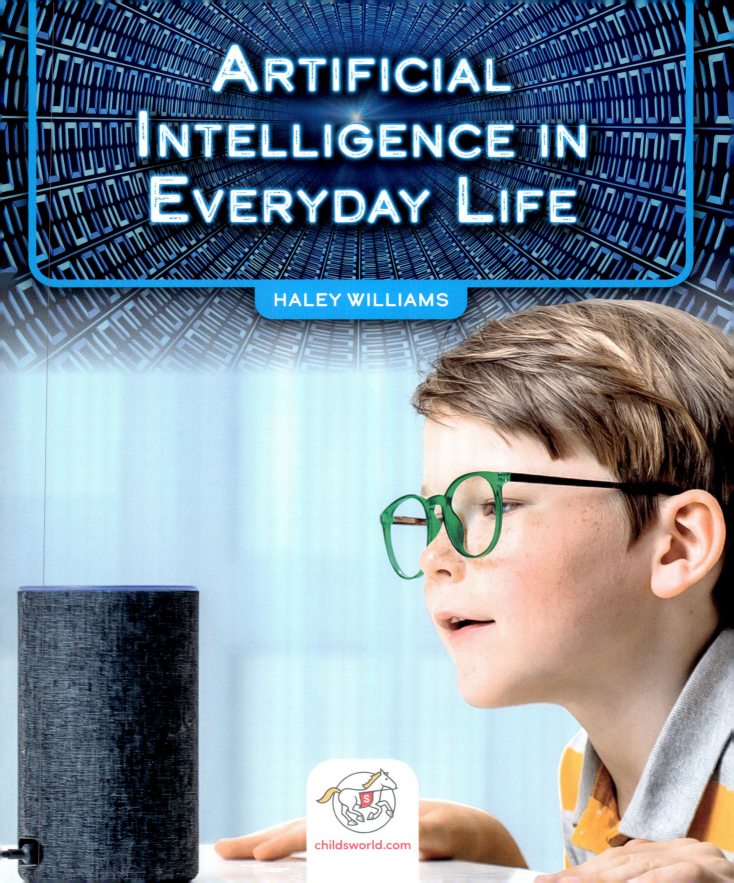

Published by The Child's World®
800-599-READ • www.childsworld.com

Copyright © 2025 by The Child's World®
All rights reserved. No part of this book may be reproduced or utilized in any form or by any means without written permission from the publisher.

Photography Credits
Photographs ©: Shutterstock Images, cover, 1, 5, 7, 14, 17, 18; Jo Panuwat/Shutterstock Images, 9; Diego Thomazini/Shutterstock Images, 10; Red Line Editorial, 13; Miriam Doerr Martin Frommherz/Shutterstock Images, 21; Design elements from Tatiana Shepeleva/Shutterstock Images and Shutterstock Images

ISBN Information
9781503893771 (Reinforced Library Binding)
9781503894594 (Portable Document Format)
9781503895416 (Online Multi-user eBook)
9781503896239 (Electronic Publication)

LCCN 2024941396

Printed in the United States of America

ABOUT THE AUTHOR
Haley Williams is an editor who lives in Minnesota. In her free time, she enjoys reading, taking walks, and watching movies.

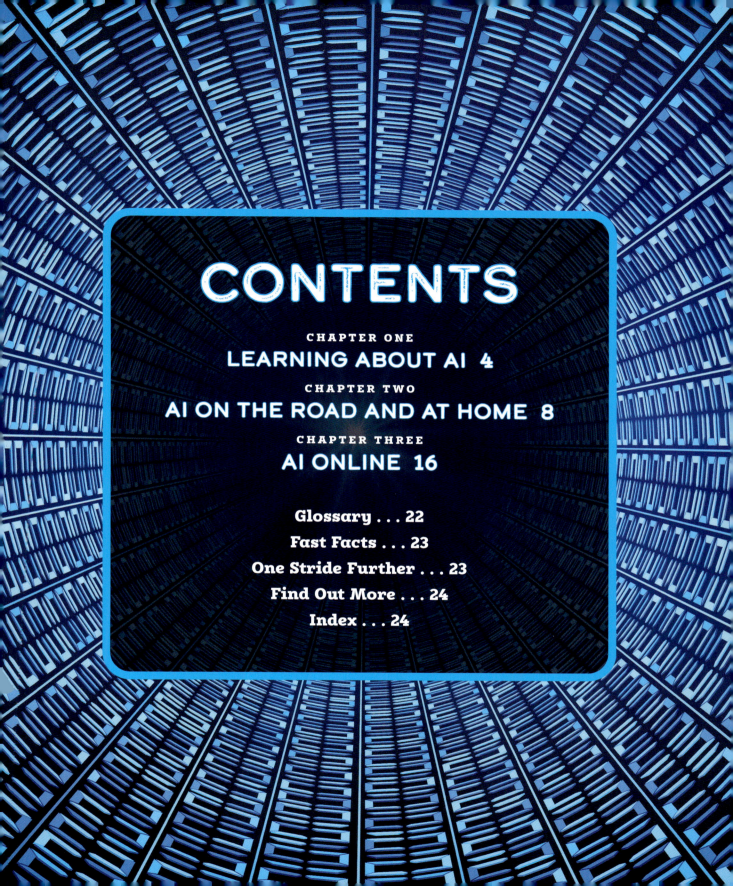

CONTENTS

CHAPTER ONE
LEARNING ABOUT AI 4

CHAPTER TWO
AI ON THE ROAD AND AT HOME 8

CHAPTER THREE
AI ONLINE 16

Glossary . . . 22

Fast Facts . . . 23

One Stride Further . . . 23

Find Out More . . . 24

Index . . . 24

CHAPTER ONE
LEARNING ABOUT AI

A taxi goes down the street in San Francisco, California. But there is no one sitting in the driver's seat. Instead, the car is using computers, cameras, and **sensors** to drive itself. The taxi pulls over to the curb. A person gets inside and sits in the backseat. The car tells the passenger not to touch the steering wheel or brakes. Then the taxi takes off toward the person's destination.

In 2023, the company Waymo started using **autonomous** cars in the United States. These are also called self-driving cars. Self-driving cars use several technologies to help them drive without a human's control. Sensors scan the area around the car. This helps the car know if a person or another car is nearby. Cameras allow the car to see street signs. And mapping systems help the car know where it is going.

Waymo cars use three different types of sensors to create an accurate picture of the world around the car.

WHEN WAS AI CREATED?

Some people believe AI is a recent technology. But early AI was first developed in the mid-1900s. Research during that time focused on how humans and computers could work together. In 1956, a professor named John McCarthy introduced the term *artificial intelligence*. And in 1958, he created a computer programming language called LISP. LISP was often used by researchers to develop AI **applications**.

Many people are unsure about autonomous cars. They worry about safety. But others believe self-driving cars will make traveling more convenient. Car companies continue to test and develop self-driving cars. And many are using artificial intelligence (AI) as a tool to improve the cars' safety features.

AI allows computers to solve problems that ordinarily require human intelligence. It also allows technology to do some human tasks, such as driving. Most kinds of AI work by collecting a lot of **data**. This data helps the AI solve problems and make decisions. As AI collects more data, it gets better at doing tasks.

AI is made up of computer programs. Programs are sets of instructions that people give to computers in languages that computers can understand.

    Today, artificial intelligence is used in many areas of everyday life. It can quickly handle common tasks. It can also help simplify people's lives. From recommending movies to providing security in people's homes, AI does important tasks for people.

CHAPTER TWO
AI ON THE ROAD AND AT HOME

Since its creation, artificial intelligence has become part of everyday life. People do not always realize just how often they interact with AI. AI is used in many products, programs, and **industries**. And in many cases, it is helping make people's lives easier and safer.

Transportation is one industry that is using AI. Some people think AI is only used in self-driving cars. But AI is used in regular cars as well. Car companies use AI in safety features. For example, some companies make special cameras for cars. These cameras use AI to check if a person is in a car's blind spot. A blind spot is an area around a car that the driver cannot easily see.

Side mirrors help drivers see objects behind and to the side of their cars. But side mirrors do not always fully capture a car's blind spots, especially if the mirrors are positioned incorrectly.

To drive safely, people check their blind spots by leaning forward or turning their heads. AI cameras make checking blind spots much easier. The cameras warn drivers if there is a person in the blind spot. These cameras could help reduce accidents.

Traffic management is another way AI is helping in transportation. Today, many cars use the Global Positioning System (GPS). GPS helps people get where they need to go by mapping the best route to take. Some GPS programs use AI **algorithms** to look for the fastest route available. To do this, the technology checks for things such as traffic patterns and weather conditions. The GPS will even recommend faster routes that come up while people are traveling. This can lower the amount of traffic in an area and make traffic go faster.

AI is also used in many technologies at home. It can help provide home security. Security cameras that have AI technology **monitor** the area around a home. The cameras can identify people's faces. This is helpful if someone tries to break into a home.

Google Maps is a popular GPS app that uses AI.

Smart doorbells have cameras that use AI to detect if someone is at the door. People can check their doorbell camera even when they are not home. They do so by using an app on their phone. If someone tries to take a package or break into the home, the smart doorbell will let the homeowner know.

Smart speakers use AI technology as well. Amazon Echo and Google Home are two examples. These devices can answer questions or search for information using the internet. They can also do things such as adjust lighting in rooms and play music or videos. The AI in these devices learns from how people interact with them. This allows the devices to make suggestions and changes based on people's preferences.

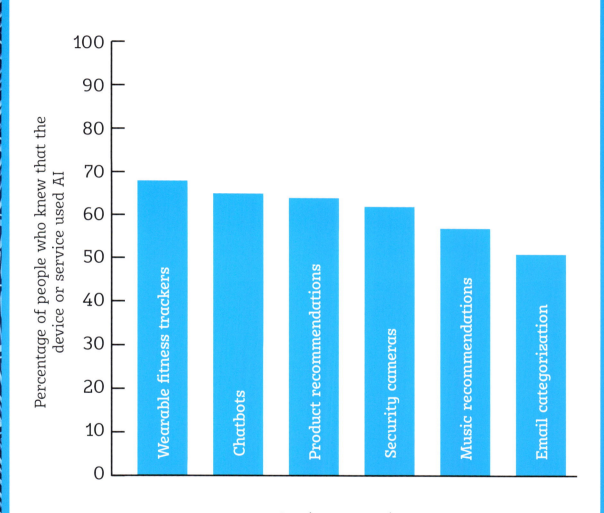

In 2023, the Pew Research Center surveyed more than 11,000 US adults to see if people knew whether AI was used in six common items or programs. Many people were unaware that these things could use AI.

Some phones scan not only people's faces, but also their irises. The iris is the colored part of the eye. Patterns in the iris are unique to each person.

Another way AI is used in everyday life is through smartphones. Smartphone cameras can recognize people's faces. Some phones only unlock after scanning the owner's face. This helps protect important information. When people are texting, AI will predict what they are going to type. It uses algorithms to guess what they might be trying to say. AI will also correct the user's spelling. Smartphones even have features that add events and appointments to people's calendars for them. Experts continue working to improve AI. This could make more everyday tasks simpler and faster for people.

AI AND HEALTH

Fitness wristwatches monitor things such as people's activity levels and sleep habits. People can use that information to track progress toward their health goals. Some fitness watches go a step further by using AI. These watches can recommend workouts to their owners. They also suggest taking breaks if a person's heart rate is high for a long time.

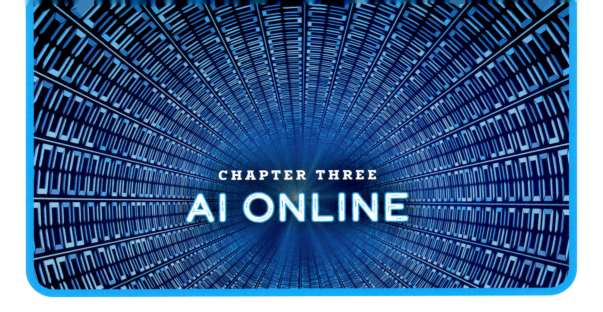

CHAPTER THREE
AI ONLINE

People also use AI on the internet. AI plays a major role in recommending content to people online. This content includes shows and movies. AI can even create new content.

Streaming services such as Netflix and Hulu use AI algorithms to make finding new shows easier. AI collects data on the shows that people like and dislike. Then, when people are looking for something new to watch, AI gives recommendations based on the data it collected. It uses its knowledge of what people have previously watched to estimate how likely it is that they will enjoy another show or movie. This helps people find the content they want.

In May 2024, Netflix offered more than 7,000 movies, series, and other titles to its US users. The service's AI recommendation system helped users find the content that appealed to them.

The first chatbot was invented in 1966. It could only handle simple conversations. Since then, chatbots have greatly improved and can handle more complicated interactions.

AI recommendation systems usually use a kind of AI called machine learning. Machine learning allows computers to learn from the data they are given. YouTube is another site that uses machine learning to recommend videos based on what people have watched before. YouTube looks at lots of data when deciding what to recommend. It looks at how long people watch a video. It also looks at the number of likes and comments a video has earned. The site uses this and other data to make a person's page fit her interests.

Chatbots are another form of AI online. A chatbot is a computer program that can hold a humanlike conversation. Chatbots help people find answers to questions quickly without having to do further research. Websites may have a chatbot on their page to help answer people's questions. Some chatbots are very simple. They are prepared to answer only certain questions. This means they may not be able to answer more complicated questions.

Other chatbots can hold complex conversations. These chatbots learn information as they talk with people. They use that information to respond to people's questions. This kind of chatbot uses generative AI. Generative AI uses algorithms that can generate, or make, new content. This includes text, sounds, images, and videos.

CONCERNS ABOUT AI

Some people have concerns about AI. They worry that it will reduce the number of available jobs. Some companies may use the technology to do simple tasks instead of hiring human workers to do them. Another issue people have with AI is related to privacy. AI collects data to learn about someone's preferences. However, people are concerned that it may be gathering and sharing private information.

Generative AI became very popular in the early 2020s. One example of this technology is the program ChatGPT. ChatGPT can create text based on the information people give it. A person can type "make a grocery list" into ChatGPT. The program will then create a grocery list. However, ChatGPT can make mistakes. Sometimes it produces false or inaccurate information.

Stable Diffusion is a generative AI that can create images. People give Stable Diffusion a short text prompt asking for a picture of something. Then, the AI creates a new image based on the images it was trained on. People use Stable Diffusion to create pictures that look almost like photographs.

Some artists use generative AI as a part of their own creativity. Others argue that AI creations do not truly count as art.

People are worried about generative AI's ability to make new content. They are afraid that people will rely too much on using generative AI to create things. Some artists are concerned about generative AI, too. They worry that other people could use AI to copy their unique style without permission.

AI has come a long way from where it first began. It has become an important tool that many people use daily. AI will continue to improve as more people, businesses, and industries begin using it.

GLOSSARY

algorithms (AL-guh-rith-umz) Algorithms are step-by-step instructions used to solve a problem or perform a task. AI uses algorithms to help make personalized recommendations for people.

applications (app-lih-KAY-shunz) Applications are computer programs that perform certain tasks. The computer programming language LISP was used by researchers to develop AI applications.

autonomous (aw-TAH-nuh-muss) Something is autonomous if it is able to act without human control. Many people are worried about the safety of fully autonomous cars.

data (DAY-tuh) Data is information collected for a purpose. AI collects people's data and uses it to make recommendations.

industries (IN-duh-streez) Industries are groups of businesses and organizations that produce similar products. AI has been used in many products, programs, and industries.

monitor (MAW-nih-tur) To monitor something means to keep watch over it. Security cameras that use AI monitor the area around homes to look for people breaking in.

sensors (SEN-surz) Sensors are devices that detect information from the real world, such as light or heat. Self-driving cars use sensors to check for objects around them.

FAST FACTS

- Artificial intelligence (AI) allows computers to solve problems that ordinarily require human intelligence.

- People use AI in everyday life. AI can make certain tasks easier and safer for people.

- Transportation is one industry where AI is being used. AI is used in car safety features and to help with traffic management.

- People can interact with AI at home. Smart doorbells, security cameras, and smart devices can all use AI.

- AI helps people find the online content they want. It recommends videos, shows, and movies based on what people have watched before.

- Chatbots can hold humanlike conversations and answer people's questions. Some chatbots, such as ChatGPT, use generative AI to make new text based on what it has learned.

ONE STRIDE FURTHER

- What are self-driving cars? Why are some people worried about these kinds of cars being on roads? If a self-driving car causes an accident, who might be at fault?

- What are some ways that artificial intelligence is used in homes?

- Do you think AI will continue being incorporated into other areas of everyday life? Explain why or why not.

FIND OUT MORE

IN THE LIBRARY

Kulz, George Anthony. *What Is Artificial Intelligence?* Parker, CO: The Child's World, 2025.

Martin, Emmett. *Self-Driving Cars: Transportation of the Future*. New York, NY: Gareth Stevens, 2023.

Williams, Dinah. *Artificial Intelligence*. New York, NY: Starry Forest Books, 2021.

ON THE WEB

Visit our website for links about artificial intelligence in everyday life:

childsworld.com/links

Note to Parents, Caregivers, Teachers, and Librarians: We routinely verify our web links to make sure they are safe and active sites. So encourage your readers to check them out!

INDEX

AI in cars, 4–6, 8–11
AI in home devices, 7, 11–13

chatbots, 13, 19–20
concerns about AI, 20–21

fitness trackers, 13, 15

generative AI, 19–21

machine learning, 18

recommendation systems, 13, 16–18

smartphones, 15

Waymo, 4–6